Preventive Vet
101 ESSENTIAL TIPS
KITTEN OR NEW CAT:
Health & Safety

S0-BCJ-669

DR. JASON NICHOLAS
Illustrated by Chuck Gonzales

PREVENTIVE VET
Portland, OR

Copyright © 2017 Preventive Vet Enterprises, LLC

All rights reserved. No part of this book may be used or reproduced in any matter whatsoever without written permission of the publisher, except in the case of brief quotations embodied in critical articles and reviews.

The material in this book is based on the author's professional opinion and experience; it is supplied here for general informational purposes only. This material is not meant to take the place of an established veterinarian-client-patient relationship. For your pet's health and safety, please consult with your veterinarian for individualized care and prior to making any medical decisions regarding your pet's health.

ISBN: 978-0-9883781-3-1

Book cover and interior design by
Robin Walker, The YGS Group

Illustrations by Chuck Gonzales

Printed in North America.

CONTENTS

INTRODUCTION

You've got a new cat! Fun! And you've likely got your hands full now, too. And so much to learn! But you don't have time to read a whole "kitten owner's manual" or scour the web for everything you need to know. Worry not, *101 Essential Tips* boils it down for you and provides reliable, essential cat care information in short, easy-to-read tips—so you can learn a few things during cuddle time, between play sessions, or even when you finally get some peace and quiet on the toilet. (Hey, I'm not too proud. I don't mind if you read it in the bathroom, I just want you to know this stuff!)

These are the tips and insights I've gathered over my years of practice and from talking with other vets and cat lovers, not to mention my own experiences of having cats (including having cats while also having kids, dogs, and an otherwise busy life, too). These tips will help you keep your cat—and your credit card—out of the ER, and they'll help you have a better overall life together, as well.

Of course, it's just not possible to cover every aspect of each of these topics in a short tip format. But don't worry, your vet is there to help, and I'm not going to leave you "hanging" either—this book also gives you exclusive access to the "Book Extras" section on our website, for when you want to dive into a topic in more detail.

One last note: *101 Essential Tips* isn't just for first-time cat owners! Even if you've grown up with cats, or had several as an adult, every cat and every situation is different and there's always something new to learn. And given all that's at stake, it's far better for you to learn these things the easy way now from my experience and the experiences of others, than to do so "the hard way" later. So dig in and may you and your new kitty have many wonderful, healthful, happy years together! Enjoy!

Dr. Jason Nicholas

BONUS ONLINE CONTENT

Extra Extra!
Learn More About It!

Don't miss Book Extras, where you get exclusive access to additional content, videos, downloads, and … contests!

Go to *PreventiveVet.com/Book-Extras*, enter this code: **1HS-66W3-7C** to unlock this free bonus section.

WANT $250 TO SPEND AT YOUR VET?
Enter our contest for your chance to win.
USE CODE: 1HS-66W3-7C
PreventiveVet.com/ Book-Extras

BOOK EXTRAS

CHAPTER 1

What & How To Feed Your Cat

1 'Meatless in Seattle'— your cat's not a fan

People, and even dogs, can get along just fine on a vegetarian diet. Your cat … not so much. That's because cats are obligate carnivores—meaning that they have a biological need for animal protein ("meat"). They can't survive, let alone thrive, without it. Not only is your kitty's digestive system designed to break down and absorb animal proteins better than plant-based ones, but those animal proteins contain all the essential amino acids your cat needs to keep their heart, vision, and immune system functioning properly. So, regardless of the dietary choices you make for yourself (or your dog), please don't try to make your cat a vegetarian or vegan. It won't go well.

2 Mice: Your cat's model meal

Your cat's "evolutionary" diet was made up mostly of mice, which are approximately 50–60% protein, 30–40% fat, and 10% carbohydrates. Now, this doesn't mean you should be serving up rodents to your cat. But it does mean that you should aim for a similar balance of high protein, moderate fat, and low carbs in the foods you feed your cat. A diet that's too far off these proportions can increase your cat's risk for obesity, diabetes, and a host of other health issues. Unfortunately, many cat foods on the market don't provide this ideal "macronutrient" balance, so it pays to read labels (and follow the advice in the next tip).

3 Kibble vs. canned

Many people believe that feeding dry food only will help keep their cat's teeth clean and healthy, but that's often not the case. The real benefits of kibble are usually convenience (can be left out longer and not as "gross" or smelly) and cost (often cheaper). However, there are far more drawbacks to a dry-food-only diet—it can actually wind up being less convenient and more expensive in the end. Kibble has less moisture than canned food, increasing a cat's risk of bladder inflammation, stones, constipation, and urinary tract obstruction. Also, dry foods are usually higher in carbohydrates and lower in protein, increasing a cat's risk of obesity and diabetes. Your best bet is to feed BOTH types! Give your cat the majority of their calories in high protein, low carb, wet food—two meals daily, not just "the occasional treat." Then, provide the rest of their daily calories with a measured amount of a high-quality dry food. As for their teeth, check out Tip #46.

4 Avoid the all-you-can-eat buffet

Sure, it's convenient to just dump an unmeasured amount of kibble into a bowl, and then top it off when it gets low or empty. However, there are lots of downsides to this method of feeding. The ever-pleasant "scarf-and-barf" and a greater risk of obesity are just two of them. But, perhaps most importantly, such a never-ending buffet makes it more difficult for you to pick up on changes in your cat's appetite. These changes can be some of the earliest and clearest indicators of pain or a developing health problem. Help your cat by measuring (or weighing) the amount of food you put into their bowl, and keeping an eye on how quickly they're going through it. Even better: give them several, small, measured meals throughout the day. Worried that your work or social schedule will make such meal feeding difficult? Worry not, busy human, Book Extras has plenty of tips to make it easy (and fun), regardless of your schedule.

Shadow hadn't been eating normally for quite some time. But it went unnoticed because the other cats had been happily eating his leftovers from the food bowls they all shared. Then mom felt his backbone one day while petting him. A vet visit and dental procedure soon revealed that Shadow's drop in appetite and weight was due to pain from four resorptive tooth lesions, a common dental problem in cats, and one fractured tooth. While his mom still leaves some dry food out during the day for all the cats to graze on, she also feeds each of the cats wet food meals before and after work every day, and pays closer attention to their appetites!

5 Not all bowls are created equal

Stainless steel is often the best option for your cat's food and water bowls since it's durable and easy to clean and disinfect. Glass and ceramic come in second, but they're not nearly as durable as stainless and can chip or break easily. Plastic bowls, while somewhat durable, can easily get scratches and nicks where bacteria can hide and result in a case of chin acne or even digestive problems for your cat, so these come in last. But it's not just the material

you need to consider: Don't be surprised if your cat has strong opinions about the size, depth, or even shape of their bowls, too. (Cats, after all, have an opinion about everything!) Some cats prefer a deeper bowl; some go for a shallower bowl. And many cats love (and benefit from) food puzzles—i.e., no bowl!

6 Portion control

Curious about how much to feed your new cat? Well, it depends on many things: the food itself, your cat's age, activity level, and whether they're neutered/spayed. It's best to start with the amount recommended on the label (or, even better, by your veterinarian), and then track your cat's growth, energy, body condition, and appetite with your vet at each visit. From there, simply adjust the amount and meal frequency as needed. It's also important to note that the "cups" listed on bags of dry food refer to actual 8-ounce measuring cups, not the cups or mugs you drink from, or whatever empty yogurt, takeout, or other containers you've got laying around. Many people don't realize this, and using the wrong "cup" is a surprisingly common contributor to overfeeding and obesity in cats.

7 Hunger games

Feedings can get complicated when you have multiple cats, especially when one or more of those cats has dietary restrictions and needs special food. The foolproof way to get everyone their specific meal is to separate them during meal times, or to stand guard and "referee" while your kitties chow down in the same room. But there are a few tricks and tools if neither of those are practical. Try taking advantage of your cats' differences. Got an arthritic or obese cat that isn't all that spritely anymore? Feed them on the floor, while feeding your other kitties on a table or countertop. You could also feed the more agile cats upstairs, or on the other side of a baby gate. Get creative, or just go shopping: There are pet feeders that only open up when the proper cat's tag or microchip is nearby.

8 How much water should your cat drink?

Just like people, different cats have different hydration needs. Your cat's water intake depends on their size, diet, activity level, and overall health—along with the weather, humidity, and several other factors. In general, cats should consume about 3.5–4.5 ounces of water per 5 pounds of body weight per day. Of course, it is possible to have too much of a good thing … even water. If your cat is drinking more than 7.5 ounces of water per 5 pounds of body weight per day, they could be showing signs of a health condition such as diabetes, kidney disease, hyperthyroidism, or other problems. If you think your cat is drinking too much water, it's time for a visit to your vet.

oliver an overweight, 6-year-old shorthair had been drinking a lot more water than usual. On top of his increased thirst, he was also "peeing up a storm" (as his owner said). Though Oliver seemed to be otherwise OK, his owner thankfully brought him in for a check-up. Catching Oliver's diabetes early meant he not only avoided a more serious medical emergency (diabetic ketoacidosis), it also meant that his diet change and insulin treatment could be started sooner. Because of this, Oliver's diabetes went into remission after just five months.

9 From desert to oasis

Your cat's desert heritage gave them kidneys that are highly efficient at conserving water. But for your cat's optimal health and wellness, it's important that you do all you can to protect them from dehydration. Along with feeding canned food (to which you can even add a bit more water), you should also put out several different fresh water sources throughout your home, and especially in the rooms where your kitty loves to hang out. Use bowls of all different sizes and depths, and perhaps even some mugs or glasses of water—lots of cats like to drink from those. There are also "cat water fountains" available! A well-hydrated cat is at lower risk for conditions such as bladder inflammation, bladder and kidney stones, kidney damage and failure, and painful and distressing urinary tract obstruction (Tip #96).

10 Slow and steady wins the race

There might come a time when you need to (or want to) switch to a different cat food. To increase the chances that your cat will like the new food and that it won't lead to "explosions" in their litter boxes or on your floors, it's best to gradually introduce new foods over a one- to two-week period. For the first few days, mix 25% of the new food with 75% of the old. If your cat is eating well and not having any digestive problems, jump to a 50/50 mix for a few days. If everything is still going well, mix 75% new with 25% old for a final few days before switching to 100% of their new food. If they have digestive problems at any point along the way, go back to the percentages they were doing fine with and then slow down your transition or call your vet's office.

11 Tempt their taste buds

If your cat ever turns up their nose at their food bowl or goes on a hunger strike, there are a few tricks you can try to tempt their appetite. Start with some extra-stinky canned food—seafood varieties will often fit the bill (and don't be afraid to go cheap, bottom shelf at the supermarket in these instances … kitty's gotta eat!). Warm the food gently in the microwave—not too hot!—or add warm tap water. This can help bring out the stink. (Aroma is super important for cats when eating!) Try sprinkling FortiFlora®, a particularly tasty probiotic for cats, nutritional yeast, or a little Parmesan cheese on their food. These can act as taste enhancers for some cats. But take note: If your cat's appetite doesn't perk up within 24 hours, it's time for a trip to the vet! Low appetite could be a sign of pain, infection, digestive obstruction, or a host of other problems. And a cat that doesn't consume enough calories daily can wind up with hepatic lipidosis, a form of liver failure.

12 Milk: It doesn't always do a body good

A cute kitty lapping at a saucer of milk or cream is such a classic image. But the truth is that milk can easily give your cat an upset stomach and diarrhea. When kittens are first born, they produce enough of the enzyme lactase to digest the lactose (sugar) in their mother's milk. But as kittens get older and start nibbling on solid food, they produce less and less of this digestive enzyme (just like people). This makes it hard for them to handle milk of any kind, including cow's, goat's, and even cat's milk! So hold off on the milk altogether and just stick with a well-balanced diet and the occasional cat treat instead.

13 When sharing isn't caring

When it comes to pets sneaking "people foods" they shouldn't—most cats (thankfully) exercise more restraint than dogs. Unfortunately, many people don't exercise the same restraint and are often more than happy to share their food with their cats. While a piece of your toast or some of your chicken isn't likely to cause a problem for your kitty (other than adding calories and encouraging begging), sharing anything with onions or garlic in it may (they can break down their red blood cells). Sharing your sushi or the anchovies from your Caesar may, too—they can contain thiaminases, enzymes that breakdown an important B vitamin. Chocolate hopefully goes without saying, but you may not know that grapes and raisins may be a problem for cats (we know they can be for dogs, but aren't yet 100% sure for cats).

CHAPTER 1 BONUS ONLINE CONTENT

Enter tip# below at PreventiveVet.com/Book-Extras to access this information.

HOW TO READ FOOD LABELS: A guide for figuring out the right protein, carbohydrate, and fat mix. (#2)

WET FOOD IS IMPORTANT: Resources for turning your dry-food junkie to wet food. (#3)

INTERACTIVE FEEDERS AND PUZZLES: Bowl and toy options for feeding and delighting your kitty. (#4)

CAT TOO FAT OR SKINNY?: A guide on how to tell your cat's Body Condition Score. (#6)

MULTI-CAT HOME: Types of feeders to use if you have more than one cat. (#7)

HYDRATION: Tips on how to help your cat stay hydrated and how to measure their water intake. (#8)

HEPATIC LIPIDOSIS: What's that? Tips on how to prevent it. (#11)

BAD PEOPLE FOODS: A list of what your cat shouldn't eat, including certain fish. (#13)

BOOK EXTRAS

*Go to **PreventiveVet.com/Book-Extras**, enter this code: **1HS-66W3-7C** to unlock this resource*

Doing Litter Boxes Right

14 Toilet training your cat? Not so fast!

Yes, you can toilet-train your cat (and amaze your family and friends). But should you? Probably not. Using a cold, porcelain potty goes against a cat's natural instincts and it deprives you of the opportunity to pick up on early, concerning changes in your cat's peeing and pooping—which are very important to catch! And then there's the logistics, like what happens if someone accidentally leaves the door or lid closed or is using the bathroom when your cat needs to go? Your kitty isn't likely to wait patiently, I'll tell you that much! In most instances, and for many reasons, the best bathrooms for your cat are big ol' litter boxes.

15 Size matters

"Cozy" litter boxes can cause serious problems. Cats prefer, and need, spacious litter boxes with plenty of room to turn around, dig around, and do their business in. A general rule of paw: The box should be at least as long as your cat from the tip of their nose to the tip of their (extended) tail. While they'll often work fine for a kitten, most of the litter boxes available in pet stores don't really cut it for the majority of grown cats. Large, shallow, plastic tubs—like those used for under-bed storage—are often the best litter boxes you can buy.

Oscar had been peeing and pooping outside of his litter box for three months. His first vet prescribed anti-anxiety medications. A month later, medications making no difference, he saw another vet. It was during this visit that the new vet asked about Oscar's home and litter box setup. Turns out that Oscar's owners had adopted another cat a couple of weeks prior to the start of Oscar's potty problems, and they were still using the same small, single litter box for the two cats. After stopping the anti-anxiety meds, thoroughly cleaning all the carpets, and adding two more (large) litter boxes throughout the house, Oscar's "inappropriate deposits" soon stopped and everybody was much happier for it.

16 Sides matter, too

No cat should have to pole vault to get into their litter boxes. If your tiny, little kitten or older, arthritic cat struggles to climb in and out of their litter boxes, they'll be less likely to use them. Make litter box access easy for your cat, no matter what their stage of life: Choose boxes with at least one low side, or add a ramp or step-up to make getting in and out easier.

17 The more the merrier

If you value your cat's comfort and health (and your carpets!), your cat should always have quick and easy access to their litter box. But since their litter box might not always be clean, available, or easy to get to—and since cats can develop bad associations with a litter box, like if they get startled while using it or have a painful pee or poop in it—it's always a good idea to have more than one box, even in single-cat households. So, what's the right number of boxes? Follow the "cats + 1 rule"—meaning you should have one litter box for every cat plus one extra. This will make everybody happier … including you.

18 Location, location, location

Just like in real estate, location is an important factor in helping your cat love (and use) their litter boxes. Ideally, each box should be placed in a different room or area of your home—not lined up, one right next to the other. If you have multiple levels, it's best to put at least one litter box on each floor, too. Be sure to avoid loud or drafty spots, and steer clear of high-traffic areas. Tick all of these "boxes," and you'll be several steps closer to helping your cat use theirs.

19 To cover or not to cover, that is the question

Generally speaking, studies are showing that cats seem to go for covered boxes as often as uncovered. So, just this once, feel free to go with the option you prefer and that best fits with your home décor. But … be ready to switch if your cat starts telling you that they'd prefer the other option. (Don't worry, you'll know!) One special situation to note: If your cat has or ever develops asthma (Tip #94), you'll definitely want to uncover all of their boxes.

20 Eau de *nothankyou*

Getting perfumed, or scented litter might seem like a good idea to you, but your cat probably won't agree. Your cat's sense of smell is significantly stronger than yours—about 40 times greater—and some scents, like citrus, can be offensive to cats. So, while your cat definitely wants—and needs—you to keep their litter box odors in check, they're likely to be irritated (and even driven away from their boxes) by the fragrances in some scented litters or litter box cleaning products. Battle litter box odors with daily scooping, good air circulation, and adsorbent charcoal... not scented litters.

21 Let's clear the air

It's not just your cat's sense of smell that's extra sensitive—their lungs can be, too. The dust that comes off some cat litters can trigger or worsen a case of asthma or other respiratory diseases—for your cat and everybody else in your home. Choosing a low-dust litter is an important step toward keeping everybody's lungs as healthy as possible. It'll also help keep cat litter dust off your floors, furniture, computers, and other electronics, too.

22 The daily scoop

Would you rather use a clean toilet, or one where things have been left to … *ehem* … mature for a few days? Well, your cat feels the same way about their litter boxes. You should scoop litter boxes at least once a day. Not only will your kitty be happier and more likely to use their litter boxes consistently, it will also help you identify potentially concerning potty changes and problems earlier, before they get out of hand or more difficult to treat. To keep things really clean, it's also a good idea to change out the litter every week or so and wash the litter boxes with warm, soapy water about once a month.

23 Read the clumps, or urine trouble

Does your cat pee once a day? Twice? More often? It's important to know your cat's normal pee patterns, so you can spot any trouble faster. If your cat starts going less often than usual or making smaller pee clumps in their litter, they could be dehydrated or peeing elsewhere (they could also be developing a urinary obstruction: see Tip #96). More frequent urinations or larger pee clumps could mean an inflamed bladder, urinary stones, a urinary tract infection, diabetes, or liver disease, to name but a few possible causes. Don't miss these signs.

Ruby an 8-year-old Siamese, started leaving more urine clumps in her litter boxes. It wasn't long before her owners suspected something might be wrong and brought her to their vet for a check-up. Ruby was diagnosed with an overactive thyroid (hyperthyroidism) and early kidney disease. Fortunately, her problems were picked up on early enough that they hadn't yet caused significant heart problems. Thanks to her treatment and monitoring program, and her owners' quick action and the early diagnosis, Ruby's heart remained healthy, her kidney disease progressed slowly, and this beautiful, blue-eyed Siamese girl got to spend many more years happily "chatting away" with her people.

24 The scoop on poop

Cats should poop at least once every one to two days, depending on what they're eating, their activity level, and a whole lot more. Pay attention to how often your cat normally poops, as well as the appearance of their poop. Changes in poop frequency, effort, consistency, color, or odor could tip you off to problems as wide ranging as stress, digestive irritation or infection, constipation, or even an intestinal tumor. So, keep an eye out and note whether they're hitting the box more or less often than usual; whether their poops are smaller or larger than normal; softer or harder; stinkier; and whether there's any straining, vocalizing, blood, mucus, or worms when they poop. If any of these problems are present and continue for more than a day or so, it's time to visit your vet (ideally with a fresh poop sample).

25 Who pooped in my shoe?!?

Finding poop outside the litter boxes? It's easy to identify the culprit when you have just one cat. But what about when you've got multiple cats? While you could set up a webcam in the area where the infractions are taking place and wait, there's a simpler, low-tech solution: Add a small amount of crayon shavings, regular craft glitter (don't use "glass glitter"), or food coloring to your cats' food to "mark" the poop of and identify the inappropriate pooper. Just be sure to use a different color for each cat! It's completely safe, not to mention kind of cool. You can learn more about this colorful trick in Book Extras.

26 Bad cat! Or sick cat?

Contrary to popular opinion, cats don't pee and poop outside their boxes to spite their owners. (Cats really aren't jerks!) There's typically either an environmental reason (dirty litter boxes, too few boxes, recently adopted and stress of "getting settled in," etc.) or a medical cause (bladder inflammation, urinary tract infection, arthritis, etc.). Rather than writing your cat off as a "bad cat," think outside the box, and if the problem continues, bring your kitty to your vet. The sooner you do, the happier your kitty will be … and the less frustrated you'll feel. Win-win!

WANT $250 TO SPEND AT YOUR VET? Enter our contest for your chance to win. USE CODE: 1HS-66W3-7C PreventiveVet.com/Book-Extras

CHAPTER 2 BONUS ONLINE CONTENT

*Enter **tip#** below at PreventiveVet.com/Book-Extras to access this information.*

WANT TO SHARE YOUR TOILET?: Pros and cons, and a how-to guide for toilet training a cat. (#14)

CHOOSING THE RIGHT LITTER BOXES: What to look for and what to avoid. (#15)

KEEPING LITTER BOX ODORS DOWN: Tips, tricks, and tools. (#20)

HOW TO CLEAN UP PEE AND POO: So your cat doesn't use the same (wrong) spot again. (#22)

HOW TO EASILY COLLECT YOUR CAT'S PEE SAMPLE AT HOME: And why you'd want to. (#23)

SEE WHAT STRAINING LOOKS LIKE: A video of a cat straining in their litter box. (#23)

CRAYON & GLITTER TRICK: How to use color to figure out who pooped in your shoe. (#25)

ARE THEY "BAD" OR SICK?: Tips to help you figure out why your cat isn't using their box. (#26)

BOOK EXTRAS

Preventive Vet

Overall Health & Wellness

27 The great indoors

There's just no denying it … when it comes to your cat's health and safety, indoor cats have it (far) easier and better than outdoor cats. Indoor cats don't have to battle other cats or keep an eye out for coyotes, mountain lions, dogs, and other predators. They also don't have to dodge cars and are less likely to encounter common outdoor poisons, like antifreeze (Tip #100). Is it any wonder that the average life expectancy of most outdoor-only cats is only about 3–5 years, while indoor-only cats average closer to 13–17 years! Worried that your cat will be bored or destructive inside, or think that it's not humane to keep cats indoors? Don't worry, Book Extras and other tips in this chapter have lots of great advice and ideas to help you keep your indoor cat happy and engaged—even if they were once used to roaming alone outdoors.

Mitzi's owner was in for a big, disgusting surprise when yet another cat bite abscess on her 4-year-old calico's back erupted one day when the two of them were sitting together on the couch. An indoor-outdoor cat, and clearly being bullied by another cat in the neighborhood, Mitzi was suffering from the third abscess on her back in just five months!! Though her owners were able to avoid surgery with the first episode, they (and Mitzi) weren't so lucky with the next two. After this third abscess—and paying for two abscess surgeries—Mitzi's people decided it was time for her to live the good life inside. And "live the good life" she does!

28 Environmental enrichment: Awaken their body and mind

If you want to help your cat avoid stress, obesity, destructive tendencies, and a host of other problems, be sure to provide them with plenty of outlets for physical and mental stimulation. Depending on your kitty's age and preferences, you can easily enrich their surroundings and keep them happily engaged with scratching posts (see Tip #32), empty boxes, toys, and food puzzles. Or you can get a little more elaborate and build an indoor/outdoor enclosed cat patio (a.k.a. "catio"), or even set up an indoor agility course!

29 Catnip—'happy hour' for cats

Catnip can trigger a sort of "high" in cats, which can help reduce stress and make them playful. Every cat reacts differently, and about 30% of cats aren't affected at all. Try catnip as part of your cat's environmental enrichment and before potentially stressful situations, like a vet visit (Tip #42) or holiday parties. You can buy it in the store or, you can easily grow this herb yourself (don't worry, it's legal in all 50 states!).

30 Unleash your cat's inner hunter

Inside your sweet, fluffy kitty beats the heart of a hunter. They were born to work for their food—and they love the thrill of the hunt! Tapping into your kitty's natural hunting instincts can help prevent all sorts of problems, from "scarf-and-barf" and obesity to boredom, destruction, and stress. But you don't have to turn your cat loose on the local bird population to satisfy their instincts. Setting up a "food treasure hunt" around your home can accomplish the same thing. Even easier… skip the bowls and feed kitty their meals in a food puzzle (a.k.a. "interactive toy"). Making your cat problem-solve to get their food is a great way to let their inner hunter out and keep them occupied and happy!

31 Take a hike! No, really.

While it might seem like an April Fools' joke, I assure you that it's not. Though it may not be for every cat, many cats do love to go for leash walks and hikes! First, get your cat used to wearing the harness and leash around your home, then get them used to being leashed outside. The training process and the walks are a great way to spend some quality time with your kitty, get in some good exercise, and amaze your neighbors! Training a cat to strut their stuff can often be done in just a few weeks, especially if you start when they're young. (Just don't venture too far until your kitten's initial shot series is complete.) If your cat has a few "extra miles" on them, don't worry…you can teach an older cat this new trick.

Davis and his two humans moved into a new "tiny house." His people soon realized that their 3-year-old cat wasn't getting enough exercise; he looked bored and was packing on the pounds. The house was just too small for him to do much running or playing in. Avid hikers and campers themselves, and having read about it online and in magazines, his owners decided to give leash training a try. Now, not only is Davis thriving and loving his explorations, his people love the surprised looks they get as they go for a stroll or show up at campsites with their "adventure cat"!

32 Scratch this, not that

Your cat's gotta scratch—it's a normal (and important) part of being a cat. Scratching lets them "manicure" their nails, stretch their muscles, and communicate. The good news is, you can keep your cat from scratching your furniture and carpets by providing something more appropriate and enticing: scratching posts and pads. To get them interested in using their approved scratching spots, put these posts and pads in places your cat loves to hang out, have multiple types, make sure they're super stable, and get your cat engaged with toys, catnip, and pheromones

(see Tip #39). To get them uninterested in your furniture and carpets, temporarily cover these surfaces with plastic, aluminum foil, or double-stick tape, and then put a scratching post next to it. For more info on cat scratching, including how to train your cat to scratch in the right places and alternatives to declawing, be sure to check out Book Extras.

33 Don't skip your cat's mani-pedis

Taking care of your cat's nails doesn't just benefit your arms and furniture, doing so is important for your kitty's comfort and health, too. Neglected nails can actually grow into a cat's pads causing pain and infection. That's why you should regularly inspect and trim your cat's nails. Not sure of how to do it, or not excited about the task? There are lots of helpful videos and tutorials online. And, don't forget, providing plenty of scratching posts and pads will help with your cat's nail care, too.

34 Head, shoulders, ears, and paws

Starting on Day 1, begin to get your cat accustomed to you touching and evaluating their teeth, ears, and paws. Not only will this make your at-home care easier, it'll also greatly reduce the stress your cat may experience in your vet's office or, if you take them, at the groomer. As an added bonus, it will help you detect problems earlier and may make the treatment of those problems easier and less expensive, too.

Jack had a few more nails to contend with than the average cat, but then, plenty of "normal toed" kitties have dealt with Jack's problem, too. As a 2-year-old "polydactyl" cat, Jack had seven toes on both of his front paws. His owners brought him to the vet one day because he was limping. His nails had overgrown so much that two on his left paw had curled and grown into his paw pads. Sedation was needed to cut his nails, clean the pads, and bandage his paw. His big "catcher's mitt" healed nicely with treatment, and his owners have since added two large scratching posts to their home and regularly check and trim Jack's nails.

35 Scrub-a-dub-dub

Though it may sound crazy, bathing a cat can be done! And sometimes it needs to be done—like if your cat ever gets any antifreeze (Tip #100) or lily pollen (Tip #97) on themselves, if they ever get "skunked," if their grooming habits or abilities decline with age, or if you mistakenly put the wrong flea product on them (Tip #101). It's best if you get your cat used to water and the process early on in life, but even older cats can learn to love the bath. (Pssst ... Don't fancy testing your luck with bathing your cat? Try a dry shampoo or washing wipes specifically made for pets instead. Or bring them to a groomer.)

36 Bonding with brushing

Helping your kitty get used to being brushed—and loving it—can really help your life together start off on the right paw. Regular brushing not only helps prevent mats, reduce hairballs, and give you important opportunities to discover any concerning lumps, bumps, and other problems quickly, it can also help your cat feel calmer and more connected to you—and who doesn't want that!

37 Ever seen a cat lick their own ears?

Though cats have a reputation for being fastidious groomers, their ears can be a bit tricky for them to keep clean. Cats can get ear infections from painful ear mites, or from out-of-control yeast or bacteria. And allergies and ear polyps increase a cat's risk for ear infections. Ask your vet to show you how to check and clean your cat's ears, and what to look for to know if there might be a problem that would benefit from a vet visit.

38 When your cat 'can't even'

Sure, your cat doesn't have bills to pay, a frustrating commute, or "dating woes," but they can still experience and suffer from plenty of stress. There are a lot of things that can cause cat stress, ranging from changes in their home environment and routine, to getting bullied by a pet "sibling" or the neighbor's cat. Even your stress can affect how your cat feels. Hiding (Tip #82), excessive grooming, changes in appetite, and pooping or peeing outside their litter box can all be signs of stress in a cat. Book Extras has a bunch of tips and additional information that will help you help your cat "chill."

39 Pheromones: The secret language of animals

Animals do a lot of communicating through pheromones—chemical compounds that send "scent messages" to members of their own species. For example, many moms (including cat moms, called "queens") release pheromones to help soothe their babies as they nurse. Cats of all ages also release pheromones from their paws when they scratch, and from their cheeks when they rub their face against objects or people in your home. This is how they mark their territory as "theirs" and

safe, which helps to give them comfort. Pheromone collars, sprays, and plug-in diffusers can work in a similar way to help calm and comfort your kitty. Try using them around your home to help treat—or even prevent—stress and anxiety in your cat.

40 Carrier ≠ Stress

Cat carriers aren't just (super) important for transporting your kitty when visiting the vet, going on road trips, or moving house, your cat's carrier can also be a safe and comfortable place for them to retreat to and rest in your home. There are lots of things you can do easily to help your cat love their carrier, rather than view it as a signal that something bad is about to happen. You can leave their carrier out as part of their everyday environment, use pheromones, and carrier train your cat (which can be super easy, and fun!).

41 | Road trips with kitty? You bet!

Though they may not travel in cars as often as dogs, cats still do (and should) go for rides. Of course, they need to be safely restrained and properly acclimated when doing so. Restraint makes car rides safer—for your cat, as well everybody else in the car and on the road. Acclimation makes vet visits, road trips, and all other car rides, easier and less ... shall we say ... "vocal." So, get your kitty used to their carrier (see Tip #40) and start taking them for short, fun, "practice" car rides now.

42 | Minimize or avoid vet visit stress

We vets recognize that visiting us can sometimes be stressful or anxiety-inducing for pets (and people). We really do try to make the experience as pleasant and calming as possible, but you can help your kitty as well. One way is to acclimate them to their carrier, the car, and your vet's office. The latter can be done with regular "social visits"—which are all about exploration, cuddles and treats, and can go a long way towards helping to prevent or reduce current and future visit stress. Many practices encourage them, ask your vet. This is just one way you can help! There are many other tips and techniques in Book Extras—far too many to list here. Check 'em out; you and your kitty—and your vet—will be happy you did!

43 There's so much more to check-ups than shots

In fact, many times, wellness visits aren't about "shots" at all. These visits are important for all cats, even indoor-only cats. Checking in with what's changed or been happening over the past 6–12 months, the examination, and the ensuing discussion about any concerns is invaluable to the health, wellness, and safety of your cat. Cats are masters at hiding pain and disease. Fortunately, we vets are masters at detecting the signs to uncover and prevent problems.

44 The importance of vaccines

While every cat doesn't need every vaccine every year, vaccines are critically important—even for indoor-only cats. Vaccines are about the health and well-being of your cat, as well as that of all the other cats in your community. And in the case of rabies, having your cat vaccinated protects you, your family, and your neighbors. Speak with your veterinarian to determine which vaccines will help your cat, and when and how often they should receive them.

Precious's owners thought that she was "the picture of health" when they brought their 6-year-old Persian in for her yearly wellness check-up. But on her vet's examination it was noted that some of the blood vessels at the back of Precious's eyes were distended and abnormal. Her vet checked her blood pressure, which was abnormally elevated, too. Blood tests were run and it was discovered that Precious had an extremely high red blood cell count, a condition called polycythemia (a rare but dangerous and debilitating condition). Thankfully, with treatment and monitoring, Precious and her people got many more happy years together.

45 Spaying and neutering: It's not just about pet overpopulation

You're likely aware that spaying or neutering your cat will prevent unintended pregnancies. But what you may not know is that it can also tame undesirable behaviors (like fighting, spraying, and "in-heat" behaviors) and help prevent disease (uterine infections and certain cancers). Speak with your veterinarian about the procedure and when would be the best time to have it done for your kitty.

46 Oral health = Overall health

Imagine the state of your mouth if you never brushed your teeth or had them cleaned! And it's not just teeth that suffer from poor oral care; it's also the kidneys, heart, and other organs. Introducing your cat to having their teeth brushed early on can make their oral care easier for life. Good dental health can be achieved with toothbrushing, certain treats or diets (VOHC approved), and regular dental exams and cleanings with your veterinarian. Be sure to ask your vet for a brushing demonstration and other tips to help you keep your cat's mouth minty, err... I mean "poultry" fresh.

47 You can't find what you don't look for

It's shocking what's been found on routine blood and urine screening tests in "healthy" cats. Diabetes, kidney disease, anemia, urinary crystals, and many other conditions, all of which are easier to treat and manage when diagnosed earlier. Early detection can help prevent further suffering for your cat, and additional financial costs and potential heartbreak for you. All cats should have routine blood and urine tests every 6 months to 2 years—depending on their age, any changes in their appetite, thirst, or weight, and any conditions they already have.

48 (Poop) check please!

Feline intestinal parasites are common in the environment and in some of the rodents and other "things" that cats occasionally snack on. Some of the intestinal parasites that affect cats— like roundworms and tapeworms—can also cause problems in people. You can help protect everyone in your home by having your cat on a regular parasite prevention program and also by getting fecal screening exams done at your vet every 6–12 months. And while cats that have access to the outdoors are certainly at higher risk, indoor-only cats can get intestinal parasites, too: rats and mice can carry them into our homes, as can our dogs, and we can bring them in— on the bottom of our shoes!

49 Be flea-free. Don't forget indoor kitties!

Fleas are nasty buggers! Not only do they cause your cat to scratch, they also suck blood and can transmit diseases—to your cat, to you and the other people in your home! Even indoor-only cats and those living in apartment buildings are at risk of flea infestations and the diseases they can carry. We can bring flea eggs in on our shoes, our dogs can bring them in, neighborhood or neighboring cats and dogs can bring them over, and rats and mice seeking shelter inside are almost certainly carrying fleas. All cats should be on regular flea prevention; there are so many safe and effective products on the market. Just talk to your vet. One note: Be very careful with some store-bought flea products and those intended for dogs (see Tip #101).

Charlie's owners took him to the vet fearing the worst. Their 4-year-old cat had become lethargic and was refusing to eat; he was skinny, weak, and having trouble breathing. Because Charlie never went outside, his owners were shocked (yet happy) to learn that fleas were the problem. Charlie had been bringing "mouse gifts" up from the basement recently. Not only had the fleas Charlie had gotten from the mice sucked his blood, they also infected him with the mycoplasma bacteria that caused his immune system to attack his red blood cells. After seven days in the ICU and two blood transfusions, Charlie got to go home. It took two months for him to make a full recovery, but thankfully he did. His owners plugged the holes in their basement walls and now never miss a dose of Charlie's flea medication!

50 Heard of heartworms? Cats can get them too!

Heartworms are nasty and devastating parasites that cats get from the bite of an infected mosquito. While a cat's immune system is better able than a dog's to kill off invading heartworms, it can take just one or two getting through to cause serious breathing problems and even death in a cat. There aren't any safe and effective treatments for heartworms in cats, but fortunately there are safe and effective preventatives. Be sure to talk to your vet about heartworm prevention for your cat—even if your cat is indoor-only (torn window screens and open doors are an open invitation for mosquitoes!).

Chloe was a happy, playful indoor cat who lived on the third floor of an apartment building. She was on a monthly flea preventative and seemed healthy. Then she started coughing and vomiting, so her owners brought her to the vet. They never expected the news they got ... Chloe had heartworms! With no safe and effective cure for heartworms in cats, Chloe's vet prescribed rest and treated her symptoms with a short course of steroids. Her owners kept a close eye on her and brought her in every six months for a check-up. Even so, Chloe died suddenly at the age of 5. Sadly, the monthly flea medication they had been getting from the store didn't protect against heartworms. They hadn't known that cats could get them, too.

51 Post Op: Stick to the plan—even if you think your cat is feeling better

After any surgery, whether spay/neuter, foreign body or bladder stone removal, or whatever, it's important to follow your vet's orders for rest, exercise restriction, and the use of the E-collar (that dreaded cone!) to prevent surgical failure and complications. It's a relatively short amount of time in the grand scheme of things, and if needed, your vet can always prescribe medications to help your cat cope better with their post-op "cabin fever." Exercise restriction for a cat is typically best done in a large "airplane-type" plastic dog crate, or a small room in your home with nowhere for them to jump on and off.

52 Painless pilling

At some point, you'll likely have to give your cat medication, which can be quite the undertaking. But it doesn't have to be so traumatic, especially if you start training your cat for it now. Give them a small amount of a "pill masker," Pill Pocket,™ or other "stuffable" treat daily—this way they'll grow to like (and expect) that treat, and you can use it to sneak in their pills when the need arises. Or maybe you'll luck out and there'll be a liquid, injectable, or compounded option available. Just ask your vet.

53 Unpack the pounds

As it is in people, obesity is one of the biggest threats to the long-term health and comfort of cats. Excessive weight puts your cat at increased risk for a variety of debilitating, painful, and costly health conditions and emergencies. Help keep your cat at a healthy weight by feeding an appropriate (and measured) amount of a high protein/low carb diet (Tip #2) and avoiding the "all-you-can-eat buffet" (Tip #4). Keeping them active and engaged with a good environmental enrichment (Tip #28) program will help, too.

54 Does your cat need sunscreen? Perhaps…

Just as we can, our cats can get skin cancers and/or sunburn from prolonged or repeated exposure to the sun … even through the glass of a window or door! Fortunately, cats can also benefit from the appropriate use of sunscreen and even UV-blocking clothing. When choosing a sunscreen for your cat, avoid those that contain PABA, salicylates, or zinc oxide—these are toxic to cats, and your cat will almost certainly be grooming some of their sunblock off themselves. The areas on their body where most cats are at the highest risk of sun damage typically include their ears, their nose—and for those who like to sunbathe "belly up"—their stomach.

55 Ah…ah…ah…choo!

Just like cat litter dust and scented litters, your room deodorizers, potpourri, incense, essential oils, second-hand smoke (including the vapor from eCigarettes), and even colognes and perfumes can irritate your cat's sensitive nose and lungs. This could cause just mild sneezing or coughing, but it could also result in or worsen your cat's asthma (Tip #94) or other breathing issues. Keep the use of these common cat respiratory irritants to a minimum. And don't forget to check and change your home furnace filter regularly, too, as that's another important part of keeping the air your kitty breathes clean and healthy.

56 How many hairballs are too many?

It's a fact of life with a cat: There will be hairballs. Cats get them not only from grooming themselves, but also from grooming other cats or dogs in their home and even from "grooming" your rugs. That said, there is definitely such a thing as too many hairballs, and that often means an underlying medical problem. Putting butter on their nose or giving them a "hairball formula" food may help to reduce hairball numbers, but they do nothing to treat and help the underlying problem. If your cat is hacking up more than one hairball per week, it's time for a vet check-up. Oh, and … watch your step getting out of bed!

57 How much up is OK to chuck?

Cats vomit. It's pretty normal, right? Well, vomiting isn't really as normal for cats as many people think; nor is it typically the result of eating too fast. Hairball vomiting is covered in Tip #56, but what about when it's not hairballs? If your cat is routinely bringing up their food more than two times per month, that's excessive and abnormal. Even a cat that vomits that "infrequently" likely has a dietary, intestinal, pancreatic, kidney, hormonal, or other health problem. What's more, not all vomiting is actually vomiting. Sometimes it's regurgitating, which is a whole other can of worms (speaking of vomiting). Either way, if your cat is experiencing "deja food" more than twice a month, don't ignore this important warning sign. Work with your vet to figure out the cause and get your cat feeling better.

CHAPTER 3 BONUS ONLINE CONTENT

*Enter **tip#** below at PreventiveVet.com/Book-Extras to access this information.*

MAKE AN OUTDOOR CAT HAPPY INDOORS:
Step-by-step how-to guide. **(#27)**

ROCK YOUR CAT'S WORLD: Easy ideas to make your cat's environment awesome! **(#28)**

CATNIP: How to grow and use it, and why you should. **(#29)**

MAKING MEALTIME FUN: Ways to unleash your cat's inner hunter. **(#30)**

OUTDOOR ADVENTURES: Tips and ideas for safe outdoor explorations. **(#31)**

SCRATCH THIS!: Tips to help you direct your cat's scratching. **(#32)**

SCRATCHING POSTS:
How to choose the best ones. **(#32)**

HOW TO BATHE YOUR CAT:
Video guide on how and what tools to use. **(#35)**

WANT **$250** TO SPEND AT YOUR VET? Enter our contest for your chance to win. USE CODE: 1HS-66W3-7C PreventiveVet.com/ Book-Extras

CLEANING CAT EARS: A guide on how, what to use, and when NOT to clean them. (#37)

CAT STRESS: How to recognize it, how to avoid it, and how to overcome it. (#38)

CAT SCENTS: A guide on pheromones and how they can help your cat. (#39)

LOVE-CRATE RELATIONSHIP: Tips to help your cat to love their carrier. (#40)

'ROAD WARRIOR': How to buckle-up kitty safely for car travel. (#41)

BE FLEA-FREE: Tips and recommendations to ensure flea-free pets and homes. (#49)

DIABETES...YES, CATS GET IT: Info and tips to prevent feline diabetes. (#53)

HARMFUL SCENTS: List of scents that are dangerous for your kitty and a video of how cats cough. (#55)

HAIRBALLS: How to figure out if it's a hairball or something else! (#56)

BOOK EXTRAS

Go to *PreventiveVet.com/Book-Extras*, enter this code: **1HS-66W3-7C** to unlock this resource

CHAPTER 4

Cat-Proofing & Keeping Kitty Safe

58 Shelter from the storm

Whether it's home renovations, a holiday party, or even just kids running around inside, changes in activity level around the home can spell chaotic times for your cat. Such chaos increases your cat's risk of injury, illness, and even bolting out of a door or window. When activity spikes in your home, you can help keep your cat safe and decrease their stress by putting them in a room or area that's off-limits to others. This can be a closed-off bedroom, bathroom, laundry room, or even the basement. Just be sure to pet-proof the area and give them a clean litter box, fresh water, and a few comfy places to rest and perch. You might also consider using a pheromone diffuser (Tip #39), a food puzzle, and empty boxes … cats LOVE boxes!!!

59 'Risky Business'

Planning a little overnight trip? Fantastic! Everybody needs (and deserves) a bit of time away. If you plan to leave your cat at home, just don't forget about their health and safety while you're gone! It can be risky to leave them alone without supervision, even just for 24 hours or a "quick weekend." From urinary tract obstruction (Tip #96) to getting injured or lost, or even becoming dehydrated after getting trapped in a closet … a lot can go (and has gone) wrong in 24–48 hours with "home alone" cats. Instead, get a pet sitter or someone else you trust to stay in your home, or at least come by each day (ideally twice a day) to feed meals, scoop the boxes, and play with your cat. (It's important for them to actually SEE your cat at each visit, to really know that nothing's wrong.) Though this may cost you a few bucks, it'll help keep your cat much happier and safer while you're away, and could make your return home much less stressful and expensive, too.

Panther's owners had just spent a relaxing anniversary weekend away, but returned home to an unpleasant surprise: Their 3-year-old cat had vomited throughout the house. Their surprise turned to concern when they noticed that he was acting "sluggish" and hadn't eaten much of the food they had left out. They took him straight to the Animal ER, where the vet noted that his bladder was distended and firm, and told them that Panther's kidney blood values and potassium were high. Their concern quickly turned to fear, as they learned more about urinary obstruction—the cause of Panther's vomiting and "sluggishness." It took two catheters, five days of hospitalization, and more than $3,500 before Panther was stable and could pee on his own again. He now gets wet food twice a day and has a live-in pet sitter whenever his people go on any overnight getaways.

60 Reunited and it feels so good

Because they're easy to see and read, ID tags are the quickest way for someone to identify and return your cat should they ever sneak out or get injured or lost. All cats should wear them. But ID tags aren't foolproof—they can wear down and fall off. So, your cat should always have two forms of ID. A microchip is an extremely important and reliable back-up form of identification for pets—including indoor-only cats. Your vet can "chip" your cat during their spay/neuter procedure, or at any other time. Just be sure to register the chip, keep your contact information up to date, and have your veterinarian scan and check the chip at your cat's wellness visit each year.

Safety note about ID tags: Consider ID tags that lay flat on your cat's collar, as dangling tags can get caught between the boards of decks, on fences, and other objects in and around your home and yard, potentially causing panic and strangulation.

Willow's family never forgot her, but they certainly didn't think they'd ever see her again. Their 3-year-old cat had run through an open door when their Colorado house was being renovated. They hung "lost cat" posters and searched their neighborhood and local shelters for months. When she didn't turn up, they assumed she had been hit by a car or eaten by one of the many coyotes that frequented their neighborhood—the exact reasons she was an indoor cat in the first place. Thankfully their assumptions were wrong. Nearly five years after she went missing, the family received a call from Animal Control in New York City: Willow had been found, alive and well ... more than 1,700 miles away!! It was her microchip that helped to reunite this far-from-home feline with her family. While their renovations were completed several years before, it was only after getting Willow back that her family said their house felt like a home again.

61 Glow-in-the-dark kitty

If you let your cat outside on their own, there's always a chance—even with your best intentions—that they'll still be outside when the sun goes down. Though your cat has excellent night vision, many drivers don't. To help protect your cat, be sure that their collar and tags are reflective. Unlike dogs, it's not really practical to put an LED or glow collar on your cat. They do exist, but since you need to turn them on, and you'd need to see your cat before the sun goes down to do so, it'd be far safer to just bring your cat in for the night anyway.

62 Knock, knock. Who's there?

Cats that are outside during the colder months frequently seek warmth under the hood of a recently turned off car, oftentimes falling asleep on the engine. As you can likely imagine, there is a serious danger if they're still snoozing when the car is next started up. To keep all cats safe—whether it's yours, a neighbor's, or any local strays—get in the habit of knocking on your hood and honking your horn before starting your car whenever it's cold outside. Otherwise, it could be a very rude awakening for you both.

63 Tempting trash

Cats are curious and playful, and they've got a great sense of smell, too! All of which often leads kitties straight to the household trash and the dangerous "treats" lurking inside, such as food scraps, empty food bags, and the trussing string from a holiday bird or roast. To keep your cat out of trouble, and the Animal ER, use sturdy, covered trash cans and keep them out of kitty's reach behind closed cabinets or doors. And don't forget about your bathroom doors and wastebaskets … cats love dental floss, but it's not kind to their intestines (Tip #68).

64 Suffocation: Bins and bags

Hundreds of dogs suffocate and die in chip, cereal, treat, and other snack food bags each year, and it happens to cats, too, though not as often. But because they're good jumpers and love to explore boxes and other semi-enclosed spaces, they've also suffocated in plastic and other bulk pet food storage containers. Most cats get into these containers by lifting the lid themselves, or when someone forgets to close the lid securely. They then get trapped and suffocate when either gravity or another pet slams the lid down. In a sealed storage container, it doesn't take long for a trapped cat to run out of oxygen and suffocate. Always make sure that food storage containers are securely closed and, if your cat is particularly "handy" with their paws, keep all food storage containers safely behind closed cabinets or doors (Tip #79).

Max a loving—and loved—orange tabby, suffocated in the plastic storage bin where his mom kept her cats' food. Max was particularly adept at opening cabinets and lids, which is how his mom imagines he got into the bin. Unfortunately, either due to gravity or one of the other cats jumping onto it, the lid of the bin slammed shut, cutting off the oxygen supply with Max trapped inside. When his mom couldn't find him around the house, she figured that Max had gotten outside. As she went to get some food out of the bin to help her search, she discovered the devastating and horrible reality. She has since learned that Max hasn't been the only cat to lose his life this way; she shares her story hoping that he will be the last to do so.

65 Felines and flowers

While poinsettias actually aren't all that problematic for your kitty (really—it's an urban legend!), some plants and flowers—like lilies (Tip #97), sago palm, cyclamen, and several others—definitely are! And even those that won't kill your cat can still cause some pretty unsettling vomiting, diarrhea, and other problems. So, be careful with the flowers and plants you bring or allow into your home, and share this info with your friends, family, and florist so they don't unknowingly send or bring over bouquets that could sicken or kill your kitty. And remember, cats LOVE to climb and jump, so putting flowers up high, well … that won't truly protect your cat. Also, petals and leaves wilt, die, and fall to the ground, where even a lazy feline can find them.

66 Sit back and relax—but carefully

An ill-placed paw, tail, or head can be (and sadly has been) crushed by the weight of a rocking chair or closing recliner. Cats have even gotten caught inside recliners, so always be mindful of where your kitty is before sitting down, leaning back, rocking, or closing a footrest.

67 These shred more than paper

Paper shredders pose a serious injury risk to cats. Curious or unfortunately placed paws and tails can shred just as easily in some machines as paper does. Be safe— keep your paper shredder unplugged. If you do keep it plugged in, always keep it in the "off" position, never "stand-by" or "automatic."

68 Your cat and strings: yea or nay?

To your cat, string is an awesome toy—but if they swallow it (as far too many unfortunate cats have done!), it's likely to land them on your vet's surgery table. Swallowed strings—or yarn, shoelaces, tinsel, Easter grass, balloon and giftwrapping ribbon, kitchen twine, and dental floss—are notorious for causing a particular type of digestive obstruction we in the vet world call "linear foreign bodies." These often end in painful and potentially deadly tears in the intestines. Cat-safe toys are your best bet. But if you do use a shoelace or other string as a toy, don't let your cat chew on it and never leave it lying around. So, what should—or shouldn't—you do if, despite all your precautions, you spot a piece of string sticking out of your cat's back end? It's a long story. Book Extras has the answer.

69 Candlelight is romantic... until a cat gets involved

Cats wave their tails wherever they want and have a knack for jumping onto counters and tables with little regard for where they land or what's in their way. Many a cat has singed a whisker, burnt a paw or tail, or knocked over a candle. Several have even started house fires! Never leave your cat alone around lit candles. Better yet, keep your cat and your home truly safe ... use flameless candles instead.

70 You might find this tip shocking

For cats and kittens that love to chew, electrical cords and power cables can be quite tempting. But cats can get a nasty shock and painful burns in their mouth—and potentially a whole lot more—from chewing on these cords and cables. Electric cord shock can be painful, distressing, expensive, and potentially fatal. And, as if that isn't enough, a chewed cord can also spark a house fire! If you've got a chewer, try spritzing some bitter spray on a cloth and rubbing down the cords, or use hard plastic cord covers to keep their inquisitive teeth off.

Picatso's family had never given much thought to their laptop power cords, nor to the fact that their 7-month-old kitten loved to paw and swat at them. That all changed though when Picatso's swatting turned to chewing. His family wasn't even in the living room when it happened, but they heard the scream and commotion from the kitchen. They rushed Picatso to the vet where he was given medications for his pain and the burns he suffered in his mouth. Unfortunately, his family had to bring him back the next night when they noticed him having trouble breathing. X-rays showed fluid in his lungs, not an uncommon problem following electric shock in animals. He spent three days in the ICU recovering, the first two in a specialized oxygen cage. His owners keep a closer eye on Picatso after that, and they cover, hide, and unplug all their power cables now, too!

71 What goes up could come crashing down

It's a fact of life with cats … they love to go vertical! Unfortunately, their climbing and jumping behaviors could be costly and sometimes end in tragedy. Cats have been injured and crushed by pulling down bookcases, flat screen TVs, and even Christmas trees. It's tough to stop a kitty's vertical explorations, but it's easy (and important) to take precautions to protect them. Use wall mounts, brackets, furniture straps, and whatever else it takes to secure precarious items around your home.

72 Launder your money*, not your cat

It's a known fact … cats love snuggling and sleeping in dark, enclosed spaces. And, if it's a little warm, all the better! So, you can imagine how a recently used clothes dryer can be enticing for a cat in search of a place to hunker down. Unfortunately, many cats have suffered burns—or even died—after jumping, unnoticed, into the dryer, only to have it closed up and turned on with them still inside. The same goes for washing machines, too. For your cat's safety, and your peace of mind, keep your washer and dryer doors closed—and always take a close look inside before using them.

Preventive Vet does not provide actual financial advice. Talk to your accountant.

Bandit a 3-year-old shorthair, is lucky to be alive after his tumble in a clothes dryer. He had snuggled into the warm, not-quite-dry-enough-yet clothes when mom left the dryer door open as she ran to grab her ringing phone in the other room. Upon return, and distracted by her call, she closed and restarted the dryer. Bandit's meows went unheard, and it wasn't until 20 minutes later, when mom returned to check on the clothes, that she realized what had happened. Bandit was rushed to the vet, dazed and burnt. Thankfully, he survived and now keeps well away from the laundry room. Mom doesn't take any chances though… she now *triple* checks before closing the washer and dryer doors!

73 Cat on a hot tin ... stove?

"Counter surfing" cats are in for a rude awakening and are always at risk of burns if they jump up onto in-use or recently used stovetops. And kitties that jump, perch, or sleep on wood stoves and radiators in the summer can have a painful surprise when the temperature drops and these home-heating appliances go into use again. You can protect your cat's paws by training them to keep off these surfaces throughout the year and giving them plenty of safer, more exciting, elevated perch options instead. Another reason to keep your cats off your stove: Cats have started house fires by bumping into burner knobs and rubbing or walking across touch-sensitive controls!

74 Cut the cord

Looped curtain and blind cords look like fun, dangling toys to a lot of cats—and many take the bait! But these cords are actually quite dangerous, because your cat can become entangled and even strangled by them. If you have curtains or blinds on your windows, take a look to see if the cord pulls are looped at the end or separated. If they're looped, either add wall hooks to secure the cords well out of your kitty's reach, or cut the loop to avoid the danger altogether.

75 Have a 'closed-door policy' for houseguests

Though they don't do it on purpose, houseguests often bring any number of cat poisons and other hazards into your home in their suitcases, toiletry kits, purses, and jackets. Keeping those items off the floor and asking overnight guests to close the doors to their bedroom and bathroom will go a long way to keeping your cat safe and healthy, and it will keep your guests' belongings pee- and fur-free, too!

76 'High-Rise Syndrome' is a thing

Many cats love hanging out on window ledges, deck railings, and balconies. But they can easily get startled by a loud appliance, or enticed by a passing bug, butterfly, or bird. When they lose their balance, or miscalculate their jump, and fall, they can get seriously injured. This situation is so common that there's a name for it: "High-Rise Syndrome." Amazingly, and contrary to what you might imagine, the injuries tend to be worse when cats fall from lower heights: between 2–7 stories. This means that no cat is immune, unless they live in a single-story house or a ground-floor apartment.

77 Got a kitten? You could be their 'high-rise'!

Kittens can be quite squirmy, and they don't yet possess the dexterity and balance of their future adult selves. Their bones are also quite fragile. Sadly, many a kitten has suffered a broken leg (or two) after falling, jumping, or inadvertently being dropped from their people's arms—and this is especially true when young children are involved. Always hold young kittens very carefully, and only let young children hold a small kitten when they are sitting on the floor.

78 Don't let your cat play 'pill hockey'

Cats love to play with and bat things around. So, keeping medications or supplements out—even if they're in their vials or pill sorters—is just too risky. It can also be dangerous for any dogs or young children in your home. Get in the habit of storing all medications and supplements safely away in drawers or cabinets, and not on countertops, nightstands, bathroom vanities, or even the top of your refrigerator (yes, cats have even knocked things off there!).

Fancy a mischievous 9-year-old Ragdoll, got on well with her canine brother, Sherman, a 1-year-old Westie. Unfortunately though, she liked to knock things off of countertops. Her dangerous habit landed Sherman in the Animal ER one night, after he happily gobbled up all of his owner's blood pressure pills from the bottle that Fancy knocked off the kitchen counter. Thankfully, it was near the end of the month and the bottle wasn't very full, so it wasn't as bad for Sherman as it could have been. Fancy still loves knocking things off countertops, and Sherman would still be happy to "get rid of the evidence," but their mom is now careful to keep all of her medications off the countertops and safely out of Fancy's reach.

79 Child safety locks... not just for toddlers

Although cats don't have thumbs, many are still very "handy" at opening cabinet doors and wreaking havoc or getting into things they shouldn't. Installing child safety locks on your kitchen, bathroom, and other cabinets will help protect your kitty from cleaning chemicals and other potential hazards, such as food, trash, compost, vitamins, and medications. And don't forget about upper cabinets, especially if you've got a "counter surfing" kitty!

80 How sinks and bowls can save your cat's life

Even if you have "cat-like" reflexes, your cat's are still faster. This means that if you drop a pill or spill some liquid medication on the floor, your cat will beat you to it. And when they do, they may just help themselves to a potentially harmful snack. Same goes for pills that roll behind the toilet, under the refrigerator, or into another tight space ... you may have trouble retrieving it, but your cat won't! Regardless of whether they're your cat's pills or yours, dispensing over a sink, tub, toilet, or bowl is easy to do and will help keep your kitty safe from "medication poisoning"—which consistently tops the ASPCA's annual "Top 10 Pet Toxins" list.

CHAPTER 4 BONUS ONLINE CONTENT

*Enter **tip#** below at PreventiveVet.com/Book-Extras to access this information.*

UPDATE A MICROCHIP: How to figure out the manufacturer and update your contact info. (#60)

COZY KITTY: How to build an inexpensive shelter for cats outside in the winter. (#62)

DANGEROUS PLANTS & FLOWERS: List of plants you shouldn't have in or around your home. (#65)

PULL A STRING FROM WHERE?: Find out if/when, and how you should pull a string from a cat's butt. (#68)

CATS STARTING FIRES: True stories (and video) of pets who have started house fires. (#69)

FALLING KITTY: More on High-Rise Syndrome and a video of how falling cats right themselves. (#76)

CLIMBING KITTY: Video of a cat's climbing skills, opening kitchen cupboards. (#79)

BOOK EXTRAS

Go to **PreventiveVet.com/Book-Extras**, enter this code: **1HS-66W3-7C** to unlock this resource

What To Watch Out For

81 Hunger strike?
Why you should give in.

If your cat starts eating less (or not at all), they could be stressed out (Tip #38), bored with the menu, sick, or in pain. It's important to find out the cause quickly, because a cat that's not eating well could wind up with hepatic lipidosis, or "fatty liver disease." When a cat isn't taking in enough calories for normal body function, their body will move stored fat to the liver, so it can be converted into energy. If a cat goes without enough food for too long, and enough fat is moved to the liver, the liver cells can become damaged by the fat and the liver will begin to fail. Because of their abundance of fat stores, overweight and obese cats are at significantly higher risk of hepatic lipidosis when they go on a hunger strike. Check out Tip #11 to see what you can do if your cat's appetite goes "off," and how long you can safely do it for.

82 If they go out of sight, they should be top of mind

Many cat owners sadly believe that a cat who has suddenly started hiding is just "being a cat." After all, cats love dark, quiet places, right? Sure, some do. But a cat that's normally social and then becomes reclusive is often stressed, ill, or in pain. Sudden hiding can actually be one of the earliest, or at least, clearest signs your cat will show you when they aren't feeling well. So, please pay attention to what your cat is trying to tell you, and then get them to the vet to start figuring out what's going on.

Molly a quiet 6-year-old longhaired cat, who was generally, shall we say... rotund, wasn't eating well over the holidays. With lots of family visiting, Molly was stressed and hid away from the commotion. Yet, even after everyone left and things settled down, her appetite didn't return. When her owners finally got her to the vet, she hadn't been eating or acting normally for about a week. Her eyes and ears had turned yellow, an indication that her liver wasn't working right. She was hospitalized for monitoring and treatment (including a temporary feeding tube). After six days, and once her appetite and liver values had started to improve, Molly was able to go home. It took a few more weeks, but Molly made a full recovery from her hepatic lipidosis. Her owners worked hard to get her to a healthier weight, and they're also careful to keep a closer eye on her—and her appetite—whenever guests come to stay.

83 Straining: Deadly serious!

When their cat is straining in the litter box, many people assume it's due to constipation—a condition that's certainly uncomfortable and concerning, but not one that most people rush to the vet for. Reality is though, the litter box straining that cats are usually doing—especially if they're male—is straining to PEE! And this is DEFINITELY an emergency! (See Tip #96.) If your cat is straining or vocalizing while trying to "go," or making frequent unsuccessful trips to their litter box, they need to be brought to a vet IMMEDIATELY! If it's a urinary obstruction, immediate vet care is your cat's only shot at survival. If it does wind up being constipation, your cat will greatly appreciate the safe relief only a vet can provide. And, either way, you'll appreciate the peace-of-mind.

NORMAL PEEING

STRAINING TO PEE

NORMAL POOPING

STRAINING TO POOP

Tiger's owners thought he was constipated. They saw their 4-year-old cat, one of three in the home, straining and yowling in the litter box throughout the day. That night, they fed him some wet food with a little pumpkin to "get things moving" (something they had read about online). If things didn't pass overnight, they would make an appointment with their vet the next day. Sadly, they woke in the morning to find Tiger lying on his side near the litter box, barely breathing. They rushed him to the local Animal ER where he was diagnosed with a urinary obstruction, which, among other things, elevated his blood potassium level and led to two cardiac arrests in the hospital. The ER vet team was able to get Tiger back from the first arrest, but he sadly couldn't be saved from the second.

84 Vital signs

Knowing how to check your kitty's temperature, heart rate, and respiratory rate can help you pick up on a variety of problems. First you need to know what's "normal." A healthy cat's body temperature is typically between 100–102.5°F (37.7–39.2°C). Their heart beats about 140–220 times per minute, and they take about 20–30 breaths each minute. Every cat can have their own "normal" though, so get to know what's normal for your cat now so you can recognize when something's abnormal later. Ask your vet or one of the technicians to show you how to check your cat's vitals. And, while they're at it, ask them to also show you how to check your cat's gums and sclera (whites of their eyes), both of which can also tell you a lot about your kitty's health.

85 Video strange behaviors

How good are you at charades? Strange question, right? Well, it's not as strange as you might look or feel when you're acting out your cat's hacking, shaking, collapsing, snorting, or whatever behavior is bringing you to your vet's office. While we in the profession promise to never judge your acting skills (OK, maybe "never" is too strong a word), we'd honestly rather see your cat doing their "strange" behavior themselves. And since they frequently won't do it when in the exam room, the next best thing is to video the behavior at home and bring it along to your appointment. If you still want to show off your charade skills, by all means, have at it. We "promise" not to laugh.

86 Knowing pet first aid could be a lifesaver

Not every accident or emergency is preventable and knowing what type of first aid to provide (or not!) can have a big impact on your cat's comfort and survival should poisonings, wounds, seizures, and other problems arise. Check with your local Animal ER or humane society to see if they offer first-aid classes, or find a good online course. Note that first aid is often just that: "first" aid. Meaning that, a veterinarian should still see your cat after you've provided initial care.

87 Pet first-aid tools— at home and on the road

Having a well-stocked first-aid kit in your home, and one in your car, will help prepare you for emergencies. Many stores and online sites sell pet first-aid kits, or you can easily put one together yourself (see Book Extras for a detailed shopping list of items to include). Ask your vet about any other specific items to add, based on your cat's lifestyle and health, and where you live. It's also a good idea to pick up an accurate pet first-aid manual so you'll have a handy guide to walk you through the exact steps for providing first aid. You can pick up a printed manual, but there are also some great pet first-aid apps available for tablets and smartphones.

88 NEVER induce vomiting until you've spoken with a veterinarian

As with many things, cats usually only vomit when it's convenient for them…and often only when they're on your bed or nicest carpet! But getting a cat to vomit when you want them to …now that's not so straightforward. Not only can it be difficult to do, but with some poisons and in some situations—e.g., bleach or a battery ingestion, cat already staggering or having seizures—making a cat vomit is actually the wrong thing to do! In these scenarios, vomiting can actually cause more problems than the poison or object your cat swallowed in the first place. If your cat has ingested anything they shouldn't have, call your veterinarian, your local Animal ER, or a dedicated pet poison control hotline before trying to make your cat vomit. They can let you know if making them vomit is safe and appropriate, and can help talk you through the procedure if needed.

89 Don't play doctor—even if you are one!

"Safe for people," even for babies, does not equal "safe for cats" and many people—including "people" doctors and nurses—have unintentionally poisoned, sickened, and even killed their own cat by self-prescribing. Medications and supplements should be given to your cat only on the advice of a veterinarian. Even if you are a human pharmacist, medical doctor, or nurse, you should follow this tip, as the pharmacodynamics and pharmacokinetics of certain drugs vary significantly between species. And while we're on the subject, "safe for dogs" doesn't necessarily mean "safe for cats" either. Again, check with your vet first!

90 'Kitty colds'

Upper respiratory infections (URIs) are common in cats, especially those that came from shelters or hoarding situations, and kitties that are otherwise stressed. Like colds in people, most "kitty colds" are mild and will run their course with some rest, good nutrition, and hydration. But there are some important differences between colds in us versus those in our cats. First, your cat can't blow their nose, so you'll need to help keep it clear (gently wiping with warm, moist cotton balls throughout the day often does the trick). Second, cats with a URI can also get painful ulcers in their eyes or mouth. Third, cats should never be given human pain relievers for their "general achiness" (see next tip). For ways to tempt a sick kitty's appetite, check out Tip #11. But if your cat is ever squinting or pawing at their eye, or if their energy level and appetite aren't perking up within 24 hours (even sooner for a small kitten), it's time for a trip to your vet.

91 This common pain reliever is deadly to cats!

Acetaminophen is one of the most common over-the-counter pain relievers for people. Well-known products that contain acetaminophen include Tylenol®, Excedrin®, and most "non-aspirin" pain relievers. It's also in many combination cold-and-flu medications, as well as some prescription pain relievers for people. Unfortunately, acetaminophen is absolutely devastating to cats! It damages the hemoglobin in a cat's red blood cells, preventing normal oxygen transport within their body. Cats should barely be in the same room as acetaminophen-containing medications, let alone be given them. If you're worried that your cat is in pain or has a fever, contact or visit your vet for some safe relief.

Lucy's owner learned the hard way—nearly killing her own cat and dropping thousands of dollars in the process—that human medications aren't necessarily safe for a cat. Being a pediatrician herself, Lucy's owner gave her 5-month-old kitten Children's Tylenol® for her sneezing, decreased appetite, and fever—something she commonly prescribed for her own "under the weather" patients. Unfortunately, the acetaminophen in the Children's Tylenol® severely damaged Lucy's liver and red blood cells, landing her in the Animal ICU for eight days. In total, mom's self-prescribing mistake cost her over $9,000 ... and almost her cat's life. She now always checks with her veterinarian before giving Lucy any medications or supplements. As for Lucy, she's none the wiser and is doing just fine terrorizing the curtains in mom's house!

92 Anemia

Several conditions can cause an abnormally low red blood cell count (anemia) in a cat, such as a flea or intestinal worm infestation, infection with the feline leukemia virus, or advanced kidney disease. Anemic cats often have pale gums and lower energy, but the severity of their symptoms will depend on how low their red blood cell count is, how quickly it dropped, and the cause of their anemia. If it's been a slow, gradual decline, it may be very difficult for you to know that your cat is anemic. Fortunately, anemia is easily detected on simple blood tests, and it is just one of the reasons periodic blood and urine screening tests are important (Tip #47). Like with many things, the earlier anemia is caught, the better it is for your cat.

93 Aortic thromboembolism

Otherwise known by its acronym, ATE, aortic thromboembolism is a condition where a piece of a blood clot that has formed in the heart breaks off and travels through the bloodstream. This piece of clot travels through the cat's body until it becomes lodged, usually where it blocks the blood supply to one or both of the rear legs. This reduced blood flow to the leg(s) results in pain, coldness, an inability to walk, and then death of the cells in the affected leg(s). ATE is painful, distressing, and often fatal for cats. So, if you ever find your cat suddenly panting and yowling, struggling to walk, and you notice that their footpads are cold and pale, take them to a vet immediately. Although the prognosis may not be good, fast medical treatment is necessary to help relieve their suffering and provide them with a fighting chance.

94 Asthma

Yup, cats can get asthma! Though technically it's called feline allergic bronchitis, or FAB for them. Cats with asthma will cough* and may even have periods of (potentially very severe) breathing difficulty. Just as in people, cat asthma can be treated (even with "asthma puffers"). There are also many non-medical steps you can take around your home to help a cat with asthma, several are already mentioned in tips throughout this book (especially Tips 19, 20 and 21).

Since many people don't know what a coughing cat looks like—it's not like a cough in people— and because it's such an important sign to pick up on, we've included a couple of coughing cat videos in Book Extras.

95 Cat-bite abscesses

Cats that fight with other cats—whether it's neighborhood cats outside or their housemates inside—are likely to develop a cat-bite abscess at some point in their life (or even at multiple points in their life). These abscesses appear as soft, "gushy" swellings on a cat's skin and often take a few days to pop up. (And they can literally "pop" and ooze nasty pus … usually when your cat is sitting on your lap or laying on your bed, of course! Murphy's Law.) Cat-bite abscesses are painful and commonly cause fever in addition to a decreased appetite and energy level. While you might be able to treat some abscesses at home, they typically heal best when treated by your vet.

96 Urinary Obstruction

Urinary obstruction (a.k.a. urethral obstruction, or UO) is a very common, very serious emergency in cats, especially males. UO can come on quickly and kill fast! Unfortunately, over 70% of cat owners aren't aware of this devastating condition until it happens to their cat—by which point it could be too late. Awareness and prevention are crucially important! Thankfully, you're now aware. As for prevention, there are many things you can do. Proper litter box setup and care is very important (see Ch.2), as is decreasing your cat's stress (Tip #38). But, one of the most important things you can do to protect your cat from UO is ... feed them wet food*! The greater the percentage of their daily calories that comes from wet food, the better (Tip #3). Learn more in Book Extras and please share UO awareness with all the cat lovers in your life to help spare them and their cats from this devastation. Together we can drop the 72% unaware number to a much more acceptable, much safer level ... like ZERO!

28% UO AWARE

72% of cat owners didn't know about UO until it happened to their cat.

SOURCE: PREVENTIVE VET UO SURVEY 2012–2017; n= 2,425

Based on data collected from multiple pet owner surveys about diet and other risk factors for UO in cats.

97 Lilies—back away from the bouquet

Easter, tiger, stargazer, and the other lilies of the *Lilium* genus, as well as the daylily species in the *Hemerocallis* genus are extremely toxic to cats! One nibble on a petal or a leaf, a lick of pollen, or even a lap of the water from a vase with these lilies can cause an expensive and potentially fatal case of acute kidney failure in a cat. Putting these flowers "out of reach" isn't enough. Not only are cats incredible climbers, but petals and leaves wilt and fall when they die. Also, the pollen drifts on air currents and can easily get on your cat's coat where they may groom it off. The only way to truly make sure your cat is safe is to keep these lilies out of your home and yard. And be vigilant whenever you receive (or give) flower bouquets—these lilies are very common at supermarkets, farmers markets, and florists. Other lilies—including lily of the valley—can also be very dangerous to cats, just in a different way. Check out Book Extras for more details and a list of lilies to keep away from your cat.

Friends Don't Let Friends... Near Lilies

And it's not just eating them that's dangerous!

#LiliesKillCats

PreventiveVet.com/lilies-kill-cats

This image is available in Book Extras for sharing with family & friends.

98 Essential oils: Not essentially safe

Please be careful if you use essential oils on yourself or in your home. Not only can the strong aromas of undiluted essential oils cause respiratory irritation and breathing problems for your cat, but if a concentrated oil gets on their skin or in their mouth—as can happen when a cat walks through a spill and when a cat grooms it off themselves—they can wind up with significant skin and tongue burns, as well as internal organ damage. If you plan to use any essential oils around your cat, do so only in very diluted concentrations and check with your vet first.

99 Rodenticides—don't let them plague your cat

Rat and mouse poisons (rodenticides) are designed to kill, and they don't "care" whether they're killing rodents or your cat. In fact, some types can even kill your cat if your cat eats a poisoned rodent! (This is called "secondary" or "relay toxicity.") There are safe ways to use these poisons in and around your home, but honestly, you've already got the "world's greatest rodenticide": your cat! So, do you really need poisons and traps? And speaking of poisons and traps, if you let your cat outside, make sure your neighbors aren't using these in their yards or under their decks … many cats have been unintentionally injured and poisoned this way, too!

100 Antifreeze—a tasty danger!

Most antifreeze (or engine coolant) contains ethylene glycol—an extremely dangerous compound for animals (and people!). For your cat, even just a lick or two—an amount they can easily get on their paw from walking through a spill—can destroy their kidneys and be fatal. Because cats are so sensitive to the toxic effects of ethylene glycol, even the addition of a bittering agent to antifreeze, which manufacturers agreed to start doing in 2012, isn't necessarily enough to keep your cat truly safe. The best way to protect your cat from this all-too-common danger is to properly store antifreeze, promptly clean up all spills and leaks, keep your cat indoors (including out of the garage), and strongly consider using a pet-safer* propylene glycol-based antifreeze.

*No antifreeze is truly pet-safe, but propylene glycol-based products are far safer than those with ethylene glycol (even those with bittering agents added).

101 Pyrethrin/permethrins—the dose makes the poison

Pyrethrins, and their stronger cousins, permethrins, are flea-killing chemicals used in some flea (and flea + tick) collars, spot-ons, and shampoos for pets. Cats are extremely sensitive to the toxic effects of these compounds. Cats most often suffer toxicity when people use a dog product on their cat—either intentionally in an effort to save money, or by mistake when they don't read the label carefully. Problems can also arise when a cat rubs against or grooms a dog that has been treated with one of these products. There are many safe and effective flea products specifically for cats, as well as dog products that are safer to use around cats. Ask your vet for help deciphering what's best for your kitty and household situation.

Jinx, Porsche, and Alfred

three littermate cats just over a year old, were brought into their vet's office twitching, salivating, and tremoring. Their family had noticed a bad flea problem and, in an effort to save money, borrowed a tube of dog flea medication from a friend, splitting the tube among their three cats. The salivating and twitching began shortly after the medication had been applied. Making the connection, their owners bathed them to get the medication off, but things didn't improve. All three needed to be admitted to the hospital for treatment and monitoring. Porsche and Alfred were able to be discharged three days later. Unfortunately, Jinx wouldn't go home for another four days, because he had also developed aspiration pneumonia from the bathwater that had gotten into his lungs at home.

WANT
$250
TO SPEND AT YOUR VET?
Enter our contest for your chance to win.
USE CODE: 1HS-66W3-7C
PreventiveVet.com/
Book-Extras

CHAPTER 5 BONUS ONLINE CONTENT

*Enter **tip#** below at PreventiveVet.com/Book-Extras to access this information.*

'FATTY LIVER DISEASE': Find out more about hepatic lipidosis and how to prevent it. (#81)

PET FIRST-AID KIT: Detailed list of items to include in your kitty's kit. (#87)

ASTHMA: Tips on how to prevent it and how to tell if your cat is coughing (video). (#94)

URINARY OBSTRUCTION: Tips on how to prevent it and how to recognize the signs early. (#96)

LILIES KILL KITTIES: Check out our cool graphic for easy sharing. (#97)

RAT & MOUSE POISONS: Tips for non-poisonous ways to keep rodents out of your home. (#99)

ANTIFREEZE: List of coolant brands that are pet-safer. (#100)

FLEA PREVENTATIVES: List of safe and effective brands to use on and around your cat. (#101)

BOOK EXTRAS

Go to *PreventiveVet.com/Book-Extras*, enter this code: **1HS-66W3-7C** to unlock this resource

CHAPTER 6

BONUS TIPS

Preparing for Emergencies

AT THE END OF THE DAY, YOU CAN'T PREVENT EVERYTHING.

Trust us, we've tried, it can't be done! Accidents will happen—there's a reason they're called "accidents." Do your best to recognize and be aware of the dangers in your kitty's environment and become familiar with the signs of a problem. Try to be prepared and to know what to do (and not to do), but—very importantly—don't be too hard on yourself. Even when you practice prevention something could "slip through." You're only human and cats will, after all, be cats. In the event of a problem, your veterinarian, pet poison control hotline, and your local Animal ER are your best resources and they're there to help.

1 Keep important phone numbers on speed dial

Whether at home or while traveling, having the phone numbers for your veterinarian, the closest Animal ER and a pet poison control hotline programmed into your cell phone can save you time, money, and stress. And it may well save your cat's life! Also, make sure to provide these to your cat sitter when you leave your kitty in their care.

2 It's 11 p.m., do you know where your closest Animal ER is?

In some pet emergencies, time can truly be of the essence. Knowing the location of your nearest Animal ER, both at home and when you travel with your cat, can save your cat's life and minimize your stress. Don't forget to leave this information with those caring for your cat while you're away, too.

3 Emergency planning—include your cat

If disaster strikes and evacuation is necessary, you certainly don't want to leave your cat behind. You also can't afford to spend precious time scrambling to figure out who's responsible for the cats, or where the travel crates and first-aid kits are. Create an evacuation plan that includes your pets, and make sure you have a place to go that will accept them. It'll decrease stress and improve everyone's chance of survival.

4 Financial aid for the unexpected

If an emergency or illness strikes before you've signed your cat up for pet insurance or you just don't have enough room on your credit card, know that there are some third-party financing options available. Since most veterinary hospitals don't offer payment plans, these resources can help to soften the initial financial blow of unexpected medical costs. Just be sure to read the fine print and make the required minimum payments or you'll be slapped with penalties and a surprisingly high interest rate.

5 Consider pet medical insurance—sooner rather than later

The costs of veterinary care, especially for treatments resulting from emergencies or chronic illnesses, can be quite high. Luckily, nowadays, pets can benefit from many of the same life-saving treatments that humans do, and similarly, the bills often run well into the thousands of dollars. These costs increase even more with veterinary specialists, such as oncologists or dermatologists. Having a good insurance policy—particularly for emergencies and illnesses—can give you peace of mind and protect you from having to base important decisions about your cat's medical care solely on finances. There are many important things to look out for when choosing a pet insurance policy, so talk to your veterinarian and do your research. Since no policy covers pre-existing conditions, you should buy it *before* you need it.

Pudge a 9-year-old Himalayan, was brought to his vet when his owners noticed that he had started drinking and peeing more. Blood and urine testing showed a problem with his kidneys, and an ultrasound revealed the cause: kidney cysts. Thankfully, his cysts were relatively small and few in number, but his diagnosis of polycystic kidney disease (PKD) meant a lifetime of close monitoring and treatment for his abnormal kidney function would now be needed. Fortunately, when he was a kitten, Pudge's owners had signed him up for a good pet insurance policy; helping them afford the increased care and veterinary monitoring that was now necessary. With a close eye and timely care when problems arose, Pudge and his people were able to get many more happy years together.

INDEX

INDEX

ABOUT THE AUTHOR

Dr. Jason Nicholas—"Dr. J"—is The Preventive Vet. Providing pet owners with knowledge and awareness to help them keep their pets happy, healthy, and safe is his passion and his calling. He created Preventive Vet in 2011 to ensure that pet owners everywhere would have reliable information, advice, and the tools they need to best protect their pets and the special bond they share.

As one of the foremost experts and public speakers on health and safety for cats and dogs, Dr. J travels far and wide to raise awareness about pet illness and emergency prevention. He is an author, media resource, and a general practice and emergency veterinarian who is happiest when helping pets and their people.

Dr. J graduated with honors from The Royal Veterinary College in London, England, and completed his internship at the Animal Medical Center in New York City. He now makes Portland, Oregon, his home, where he lives with his wife and their two wonderful daughters. Their family is kept smiling and laughing with the help of their superdog, Wendy, and ever-cool cat, Smudge.

Welcome to the Preventive Vet community... where pets are protected and celebrated!

We're not just about helping you avoid pet hazards and dangers, we also love celebrating the relationships between pets and their people and the many joys that pets bring to the world. So come join us and other pet lovers on our website and social pages. Interact, get more tips, and share your stories. You can even post a pic of your cat enjoying their *101 Tips* book!

Sniff around and check us out!

 PreventiveVet.com

 instagram.com/PreventiveVet

 fb.com/PreventiveVet

 pinterest.com/PreventiveVet

 @PreventiveVet

 youtube.com/PreventiveVet

Did you enjoy and learn something new from this book? Do you think other cat lovers would benefit from the book? Please take a moment and give it a review: PreventiveVet.com/Book-Review

NOTES